A Mnemonic For Desire

A MNEMONIC FOR DESIRE

Poems

STEVE MUESKE

GRP

Ghost Road Press
Denver, Colorado

Published in the United States of America.
First edition.

Library of Congress Cataloging-in-Publication Data.
Mueske, Steve. (1965—).
A Mnemonic For Desire.
Ghost Road Press
ISBN 0-9771272-9-x (Trade Paperback)
Library of Congress Control Number: 2005937313

Book Design: Sonya Unrein
Cover Photo by Elena Ray

Ghost Road Press, Denver, Colorado
ghostroadpress.com

Acknowledgments

The poet would like to acknowledge the following online and print journals in which these poems first appeared.

88, The Alsop Review: Anthology One, The American Poetry Journal, Blaze, Blue Earth Review, Botteghe Oscure, Can We Have Our Ball Back, Diner, Eclectica, The Eleventh Muse, For Poetry, Fulcrum, Hogtown Creek Review, The Left Bank Review, The Massachusetts Review, Miller's Pond, MiPoesias, The New Hampshire Review, New Works Review, Northeast, Octavo, Pierian Springs, Poet Lore, Rattle, Redactions, The Red River Review, SalonDAarte, Snow Monkey, The South Dakota Review, The Tusculum Review, Tryst, Water~Stone, Whistling Shade, and *The Wisconsin Review.*

Several of these poems also appeared in the chapbook *Whatever the Story Requires.*

In addition, the following poems appeared in these anthologies:

"Today at the Bureau of Joy," in *Hymns to the Outrageous: An American Poetry Sampler*

"After Reading of an Amazing Device That Brings Back the Dead in Lifelike Holographic Images," in *The Alsop Review Anthology One*

"On Poetics," *The Best New Poets 2005*

"Nocturne," *Anemone Sidecar*, an e-book from Ravenna Press

"On Desire," *The Bedside Companion to the No Tell Motel*

Dedication

To my wife, Becky, and daughters Tess and Natalie, without whom none of this would be possible

Special Thanks

Sonya and Matt, Joe Millar, Dorianne Laux, Judith Barrington, Jim Moore, Patricia Kirkpatrick, Deborah Keenan, Roberta Hill, Mary Rockcastle, Sheila O'Conner, Roseanne Lloyd, RJ McCaffery, Amy Unsworth, Steve Schroeder, Ryo Yamaguchi, Kathy Weihe, Frank Matagrano, Chris Potter, Jaimes Alsop, Rachel Dacus, Claudia Grinnell, Jeff Bahr, the poets in the private workshop of three candles and Haven, and the poets at the public workshops of The Gazebo and QED.

Contents

I

This Far in August

Are wildflowers holy? Are weeds?
There's infinite hope
if both are, but perhaps not for us.
—Stephen Dunn

i.)

By now the bull thistles
have become legends

of defense, claiming
space among the wild daisies,
larkspur and mustard
by the simple
untouchable violence of form.

They tower over
their neighbors, guarding
their weedy plots
with a sense of drama.

Every wild weed sees this
and knows, they, too,
have put down roots;
they, too, have a stake in artifice.

ii.)

Summer has crossed
its apex, every living thing
logy with heat and sunlight.

Smartweeds cling to fences,
gangs of leafy spurge
spread over the hills,
and violets, those
lovely muses, sing whenever
the wind shifts.

Every wild weed
has provided for itself
beyond the pale
of spray or blade.

Every wild weed
believes it has only one season,
one season only.

iii.)

The Karner Blue butterfly,
so near extinction, does not care
about the strength
of muscled stalk and toothy leaves.

It knows only the pang
of hunger and the freedom
of a new season with wings.

The humid air
swaddles flower and butterfly.
Within days the purple whitens

with seed. Wind blows them
to neighborhoods
where they are not wanted,
but where some will,
despite the odds, survive.

At Roughlock Falls

Here where water meets water
tumbling down
from the moss-covered heights
is a pool of shadows and
a blue arc smashed into mist.
Sunlight swathes the nurled orange walls
greened with lichen. Tree
and plant roots dangle from earth's-edge
in tangled braids, like witches' hair,
roots of alien vegetables, strange
eroded scalp. The sound
is a susurrous roar
of making and unmaking, the earth
having long ago lost
its fingerhold on soil over bedrock
washed downstream. It is
a quiet way, this way
of water following the ancient
earth-pull of water to water,
however many miles: dodges
through trees, arterial races
over plains, the free-form ballet
over curved and swollen lips
wherever rocks wait below
on the river's progress to the Gulf.
It is a quiet way, this way
of water—until, tumbling
down from the greenish heights,
it is broken and remade,
in perpetuity
shouting: *hush.*

The Morning I Become Ombudsman to the World

Behind this drawn curtain
I cast my ballot, secretly
throw in my lot with all those naked

renegades of joy who sing
in the shower. Here on the porcelain stage
diamonds flash on droplets, gifts

from the orange spotlight
low in the sky. I love
this window, and the ritual of watching

my neighbors enter the day
as I sculpt my body
in soap. Yes, this is the body

I've known these many years, though
it has betrayed me
often enough. I attend these knobs and rises,

and purplish scars, model
blades and buttocks—all while bellowing,
in my perfect pink glory,

to the deaf and silent multitudes.
And when done, I will go out
into the world, to love it, unequivocally,

in all its belching verdure, its endless
complaining. After all,
I was the only one present

when the votes were tallied,
and I might as well begin by taking
that first official step.

To the Black and Yellow Spider in My Garden

You there, in your silken hammock
strung up in the black-eyed susans,
what a life it must be to lie in the sweet spot
waiting for the breeze to bring your lunch,
some hapless blowfly or loitering gnat.
You've the best place in the yard,
with only the neighbor's cat to worry about,
a slideshow of alliums and hibiscus
for an afternoon's entertainment. You are a drifter
with a long history of traveling, black-masked,
through green countries of bluegrass.
One hint of trouble and you drop and roll
beneath the hostas, peer out with fangs bared.
And then it's on again, some new place
to set up shop. How handy it must be
to carry around your livelihood, your craft,
in a single well-made suit. What a life,
this going place to place, this daily setting out
to remake the wheel: each time
you get a little closer to perfection.

"a small blue god"

Today, he's playing a toy piano
atop the dump. It's Tuesday and he's safe

because the washer women are out
degreasing the clouds. *Valderee,* he sings,

valderah, his tiny voice nearly
buried beneath the scavengers' *crees.*

He might be the smallest of all gods, the least
likely to bring change. Yet every day

he sings to the sky because it looks
so much like him, big and full of hope.

After Reading of an Amazing New Device That Brings Back the Dead in Lifelike Holographic Images

—*Weekly World News*, 7/15/2003

Someone has left the box on again, and there Aunt Mertle
bends to the bright task of baking rhubarb pies. She wipes a hand
on her apron, looks toward the stairs where those still alive

have dropped anchor, their little dream boats afloat
in the wide lake of sleep. And soon Uncle Fred,
dead these seventeen years, is done splitting wood for the fire,

hands folded over the ax-head in that moment
following work when the muscles still sing
and the mind is freed from the habit of motion.

How young these habitués of the laser look, how comforting
and familiar. Here cousin Matthew will never know
the slice of a boat propeller, and Anne can safely ignore

those pricks of pain in her arm. After two weeks at the lake,
he's mowing the lawn's shaggy hair, and she's sitting
at her desk overlooking the wildflowers,

organizing a protest to save the city's trees. Meanwhile,
the stars of another decade swing round the house
and slowly disappear in the orange flame of early light.

At the Lightning Strike Survivor's Support Group

Who could believe such dumb luck
as to hear *Agnus Dei* after the white clutch releases,
when you are face down in the culvert,
cold rain muzzling your neck,
air pricked with the scent of—what is it? dog lips?
You stand up on dead, stone-ancient legs,
soaked clothes seeped to skin,
and walk the three miles home. It is dark,
colder than obsidian. The moon is
nowhere to be found. Who would believe
such a story, the odds of being struck
by a million-watt nerve hammer?
Or later: the muse of muscles
and lesser viscera slowly letting go
its cellular charge: your hand
become thing, heart the accordionist
of the *Sagra della Bistecca*
that year you fell in love with
a green-eyed girl from the vineyards.
Now you're gathered in the YMCA
with those few who understand that twinning
sense of luck and loss,
death come and averted, the rushing itch
of ignition. *I was pinning laundry when,*
the woman from South Dakota says,
and touches the pinkish scar
that travels ear to ankle like a testament
of chance, alchemic burn of circumstance.
You want to talk about your arm
as that arm, how it dangles
like a washrag, how on some days
you'd rather just cut it off
and be done with it. But you stare
out the window at the rain, struck
by a vision of loneliness: minutemen sleeping
in their silos, each wearing
a ninety-ton night cap of concrete.
You think about the air command's
symbol of hands holding lightning: *deterrence*

through strength. Was it easier to sleep
knowing the ruin of the world
was in someone else's hands? Imagine
the isolation of two soldiers
ensconced in an underground room,
their every move a trained stop gap for liftoff —
that 65,000 pound hammer, bleeding
fire, headed toward some nexus of unmaking
on the other side of the world, warhead
singing like that otherworldly turn
one minute and twenty-four seconds
into Barber's song.

44th Street Avatar

This evening rush hour
a boy is dancing on an overpass
above four lanes of traffic.
His body limned in light,
his hands weave in the wind,
as though he were a shirtless composer
conducting an aleatoric song for brakes,
horns and tires.

I'm stuck in the stop-and-go drudge,
imagining Moses
on the banks of the Red Sea:
a man still trying to work out how fire
could burn without consuming
as he coaxed water into walls
with the mesmeric sweep of his staff.

Perhaps the boy is neither a musician
nor a prophet, but an avatar with a taste
for the poetic, inserting caesuras
into traffic lanes below.

Whatever god he might be today,
he's still a boy who's realized
the joy he feels can be freed
like butterflies from his mouth.
I have just enough time to thank him
for the open space on my right
before I dart from world to world.

July 4th

With fireworks to our backs, the sounds of explosions
carry queerly down the path. Not one sound, gathered out
of the vacuum of air, but three caroming off the glass and steel tower
to our left and the trees to our right. More strange

still are the ripply, rocketing sounds of the sounds themselves
traveling between destinations, around the curve of the asphalt path,
swooping like a shadow here and gone, unearthly and invisible
as the angel of death rushing to its next engagement. I can feel

my baby's heart palpitate in her chest, and see her tears,
as though in this terror were the recognition of the end
of all things. Our car still three blocks away, I recall an old man
I'd seen earlier in the day, standing alone in a crowd, his hand

held firmly over his heart. While the band played the national anthem,
an ice cream vendor hollered, and teenagers nearby joked
about who they would and would not fuck. A single tear rolled
out of his left eye, followed the hollow curve of his cheek, and fell

to the earth.

Butterflies are Cannibals

—from a sign at Davanni's Pizza
listing little known facts.

For a long time
you considered beauty a thing
coiled up in your belly,
as though the act of *becoming*
was all this chewing meant.

One day, the pain
grew too strong to bear
and you stopped moving
through the world,
drew your shelter
about you like a cloak,
and retreated from view.

Curled in your green womb
your body contorted through
days and nights of metamorphoses
glimpsed only in dreams.

What got you through,
if you'll remember,
was the certainty of the day
you'd wake to blazing light,
and the world irrupting
in green and gold.

You didn't know there'd be
this hollowness in your belly,

this urgent sense of being
ravenous.

Sunday Afternoon Dialectic

I wrote:
The hawk in the blue loft, circling.

I wrote:
The hawk lofted in blue, circling.

I wrote:
The hawk circling in the blue loft.

While around me I heard the machinery
of birds—what, trilling?—from their green enclave.

And I lay back and heard them: the crickets
trilling as if about to burst from their crusty shells

and thought of Kunitz and the old willow
beating on the window pane. I looked up to see

the hawk in a throw of blue sky—wings trembling
on a tide of air—circle tighter and tighter,

black eyes scanning. I watched for the head to lock
and the wings to fold in that momentary pause

before the strike of lightning.

While Listening to Philip Glass

—June 2003

Cottonwood seeds drift
like snow through the bowed legs

of highway arches. Cars on the bridge above
sound like rain passing from place to place.

I see Berryman's thirty-one-year-old ghost
looking over a bone-cold river

clouded with falling snow. What occluding loneliness
is greater than the last, greater than wind

failing to hold the form aloft and gentled
along its less trafficked highways?

Time shifts and does not. Things change
and do not. Today is gray and windy

and filled with seeds drifting like snow.
I'm sitting on a grassy knoll

below the bridge. It is windy,
and I'm listening to a few recurring themes.

A Short History of Things Not Quite Themselves

In fall the dogwood remembers
the former fullness of itself-with-blossoms,
the way a rag, once a favored shirt,
lingers for the body, the way
a bra misses its unscarred mistress,
hangs now on a hook in the dark,
where the ties used to be. Sometimes
things just aren't right—
are caught in a power outage, left
unattended or broken. It's not
always a matter of fault.
The silence is not silent.
Under the soft layers of dust
is more dust, then the idea of dust
in that tenuous layer between table
and air. Hear that? No, not
the keening of the vagabond
whose one song has the power
to raise the dead. The other:
trapdoors, unhinged and screwless,
flapping in changeable weather.
They are testifying like true apostles
to all who will hear: *It's me. Me, goddamnit.*

The Art of Measured Breathing

—For Jason

The world was cold as a meat locker,
    streets ridged with hard-packed snow,
the night Jason fell out the door
    of Nate's beat-to-shit black pickup
and rolled like an armadillo, tucked
    in his brown bomber jacket. In the theater

of my held breath, I heard bones break,
    saw his head strike the ground at just
the right angle. I glimpsed the years
    he'd be confined in bed, hours spent
looking at his body from the air above,
    but he sprung to his feet unfazed and

goddamn if we didn't laugh as he struck
    a weightlifter's pose. We walked
into the bar that night, lit like struck matches:
    untouchable. But as the layer of years
peeled back Jason found himself in bed
    anyway, immured in the muted light

of burgundy curtains. Legs that once powered
    a hi-hat and bass drum had withered
to birch saplings beneath a yellow blanket.
    Machines whirred while nurses worked
through rotating shifts. Though he grew
    to despise ALS, he got his revenge

by vowing to live longer than most.
    Some days I think he must dream of flying
out of his body, like a snowbird, invisible
    in the air over a cold field of white.
Up there: no hourly change of feeding tube
    or purled spittle sucked from lips; no

nurse rubs an arm or leg. His arms grow
    heavy with wings, a small price for the sky.
On days when even light seems freighted
    with loss, I think of the choice he made
when it meant life or death: his hours daily met
    with the measured *hish* of intake.

After Surgery

Five days back from the dead
and I'm touching my face in the mirror.
Can this be me, this ghoul from the pit of knives
with his piecework of bandaged skin?
His abdomen is stapled from sternum to pelvis,
caked with blood, and smeared
yellow. I touch the catheter tube
growing like a bean sprout from my penis.
A bag of urine is strapped to my leg.
My heart is a box of mold.

Oh, but the world outside is burning
with beauty! The light that crawled out of bed
this morning will become epic by nightfall,
a story of tree bark and iris, birdsong and dust mote,
Mandelbrot penciling the edges of leaves.
The distant whirr of industry:
the mechanic's air wrench, wasps
nudging sun-warmed brick. Soon

the noise and stench of the world
reappears, trailing in the wake of buses,
in the dance of air behind jet planes.
A woman gesticulates in her car,
cursing into her phone. An old man
mourns his murdered son. This morning
the paper birch nuzzled my window
like a lonely mare. I was struck dumb
by the delicate lacework of weeds
greening a wall on my walk to work.
I kicked a rock, watched a tower crane
swing a pallet across the sky. Yes,
I am one of the lucky ones.

The Birds at the Grain Elevator

Fling the emptiness out of your arms
into the spaces we breathe; perhaps the birds
will feel the air with more passionate flying.
—Rilke, The First Elegy

The birds at the grain elevator have stopped thinking
altogether, not
that birds are inclined toward thought,
naturally, but I wonder,
watching them given over to the art
of play,
how it is that they can become
a dandelion in the wind,
an atomic cloud, or a hive of bees,
if not for some grander design.

It is
as though this were the very definition of being
alive in the sun,
and these shadows,
even these anti-bird dots
cast on long slender silos,
wiggle and vibrate
in a frenzy of collapsing and expanding
circles of pleasure.

There is something about freedom here,
and something about cycles,
and nature,
and the impending sense of winter
approaching.

This is the dance.
This is the throb and pulse of heart.
This is the exercise of the chambered muscle and the eye.
This is all giving-over-completely-to-the-spirit-of-the-wind.

When one tires,
they all flock to the top and become
an audience eager for entertainment,
while another flock of birds
mad for flight,
enter the maelstrom
and roll like a wave or a roller coaster
eating up the paint-chipped wooden rails
on that last stomach-flipping curve toward home.

II

Into the Realm of Angels and Radio Waves

Rescuers save driver hanging from I-4 rail
—Orlando Sentinel, July 11, 2002

dangling
by a wish-
bone-shaped bolt

the woman sits
strapped
in her 2-ton SUV

practicing the art
of stillness

in this swaying silence
long after
her screams and the ghost of her screams
have stopped

there is a kind
of beauty

in

time suspended

the coiling tension in her arms

the naked curiosity
of souls
below

she knows now

the precise distance

between

heart and throat

having found strength in the deepest
well of will

by accident

she is conscious
of
every
vibration

every shifting nuance

of the earth's body

even
the weight
of her own breath

...
here
is
the long-sought-after
proof
of other minds:

the woman lifted out
of
her cage
and into

the realm of angels
and radio waves

there can be
no arguments
about external objects

or the sufficiency of a hand
as proof thereof

just the TV world watching

one extended hand,
one reaching hand

all of us
watching

Playing Records on an Old Zenith Portable Stereo

in the cool basement
before school began, suspended
layers high, like thin black pancakes
on the lip of a pin
the metal arm
would zap like the finger of the dead
if the power was on
you learned to load
the spindle and adjust the speed first,
the click back
to 33-⅓ from 45 or 78, those
excursions into other times with a stack
of shorts, or fat red slabs
wobbling on the turntable, needle riding it out
like a storm-tossed
fishing boat far

from fool-proof, sometimes
two would fall or the needle get trapped
in that sleek zone
between grooves and paper
whup whup whup
you'd
forget the stylus was alive
and get a good shot
of the old juice, the old nerve jive

like the time you peed on an electric fence
and got zapped with your
britches about your knees

woke in the ditch with your prick
a tiny white mushroom
in the grass

then all was all
right again, that scratchy sound
digging out the drums, Elvis wailing
Are you lonesome tonight?

while you dropped
billiard balls
into the Brunswick's pockets just
to hear the trip down the track, the

clunk of each ball
into the tray
you got so
you would load the records
and leave them for a later,
a fine layer cake to be consumed
in the afternoon hours, when you were sure
to be alone
they were found like this
when your father and grandfather
finished the basement: coated
with a fine snow
of sawdust

see how gently you washed
each vinyl disc in the bathroom sink,
drawing the first shape
with your rag, a face, how lovingly
you wiped and stacked them
and later
the grooves popped with a kind of clarity
your could only find
in the cleanest curves

Fly

All the fly wants
is out, to stop hitting
the glass and get out
into the weedy field
where all the noxious
theories of heaven are.
It's not fair. Somewhere
a pile of sweet
dogshit waits, somewhere
garbage mellows
curbside, but not
here. It rubs its eyes,
brushes its wings.
Where the hell
is here, anyway?
A hundred versions
of *there* are right there.
A bit of spit in hair,
tie straightened
for the dance, it's back
testing the will
of the material world
and betting on
breaking it down
eventually.

A Day for Yeses

open an ampoule of joy
—Thomas Lux

If a hinge is missing a screw, somewhere a shutter grieves
against a house. When open hands pause above a box,
it is time to wonder about reaching and withdrawing,
and whether hunger does make bones rattle. Smile more.

It helps the sun shake off the cold of fall's night cloak.
Leap more. Your hands were made for holding the air.
Know that if there are bits of sand in your nails, a fly
will find the open window; the boy will escape the fire.

Music can be heard in the slow drone of flowers arching
toward light, in the smooth curve of a vase, and in the small
of your eyes, where laugh lines hide furrows of eager seeds.
Looking in the mirror this morning, you were happy, the way

light learns to dance with water, the way a boat's anchor
will stay on the seabed. Whenever you feel the urge to kiss,
kiss the wind. Your lips were made for freedom, and this day,
a day for yeses, is the most important day of your life.

Kitchen Homily

One day, the last of the four wedding toasters
leaped madly from the counter in a trail of crumbs.
No one saw it coming, not even the silverware,
who usually take pride in knowing everyone's

business. The trembling saltshaker watched
as the toaster swung from its cord, pendulous
and heavy in the early morning dark, wall socket
sparking with blue fire. The small appliances,

already nervous by nature, ground, pureéd, cut,
and otherwise opened various sections of air
until the circuit blew, and they stopped, cold
and speechless. It's all come to this: the fridge's

heavy shiver into silence, the microwave's dark
on dark freedom from the tyranny of green digits,
the solid, final thump of the toaster on the floor
milliseconds before the cutlery assume control.

When Advertisers Finally Sell Ad Space in Your Dreams

You won't be satisfied
with your appearance anymore,
not when you can have *Star-Quality Hair*™
sublime buttocks, the perfect smile.

There might be confusion at first,
why, for example, a sweaty midget
appears on a unicycle holding a can
of *Pepsi* in your vacation memory,

but you'll learn to stop questioning
dream logic. Longing is longing,
after all, and they've done the studies,
they know the associations.

Think of the benefits!
There'll be no need to track down
endless meanings of the word *house*.
No books to buy, no days of worried

confusion. When you are lost
in those endless rooms, each smaller
than the last, a new house will appear
to replace boarded up walls.

Imagine a world of unlocked secrets!
You could become a real-estate mogul,
a sexual aesthete, professional saboteur.
Even a priest! Earn a degree

in your sleep! For those who prefer
unaided dreams, we offer another service:
our unobtrusive boxes with idea filters
come in a variety of popular styles.

You should be aware, the transition
back to yourself might take a day or two.
Some focus groups reported seeing
roving bands of angry midgets

lost in houses with endless rooms.
Some told their bosses that nothing
could entice them to come back to work.
At the advice of counsel, we warn you:

use caution and plan well in advance.
An unexercised mind is dangerous
and unpredictable. And really, isn't it
better to leave that to the experts?

Skating Lessons

She is young, someone's
mercy, bundled in the brittle cold.

She has come a long way across the ice, cutting
her own story in the intaglio

of curves and lines there. Someone
said go and they went, she among them,

in the new-falling snow,
in the black night rimmed with lights,

gloved hands outstretched
for balance. Her mother sits

somewhere among us, the hopeful,
watching her daughter fall,

get up and fall again. The woman's gaze
is focused on the oneiric spotlight

there, just there. She is prepared
to make any sacrifice, endure

any hardship, except failure
when it matters most.

The Monster, On Living

Perhaps it is
because lightning once tricked its blue fingers
along my spine, and called me

out of nothing
with a ghostly imperative. Perhaps it is
the itch of skin that is and is not

mine. A stranger to this life,
I am learning to read the iconography
of green. Sleepless, I move

through shadows, a master of solitude
and little else but the moveless and wide dark
from which doubt wells.

Why do these borrowed eyes see, these
cold fingers touch
the nascent heads of supplicants reaching

toward sun-shot sky?
It can't be love—for what do I know of it?
And not memory,

for I have none. Why this desire then,
this trembling to hold and to name?
And what is this anxiety

that hums in the root of all things,
that I should be afraid
to lose what I do not yet comprehend?

On Desire

If I could burst into bloom, red
with the rose of it, with the rise and swell
of it, called into being through
the deep green, and trembling with light,
I might understand. If I knew
how light touches water
with a tracery of trees, gifts
the world as it is not, I might know
why I am not a rose or water or light
but a man who suddenly believes
in witchcraft. What else
but this hollowing fire, this mark
of the thaumaturge, could make
the wild heart, so like a bird, thrash
in its cage? Imagine rain and wind,
portrait of tempest with shed: shivering
slivers of wood, the whole structure
in danger of imploding. Here under
a black sky swirling with clouds
I am ready to be unmade. The air
is charged and blue, and my hands
are burning with light.

Why These Poplars are Crying

As a child he'd dream of wild horses
whinnying in the sky. He could feel the rough leather
of their reins in his hands, his godlike shoulders

gilded in sun. When news of his death
spread through the world, pilgrims came to say goodbye.
The daughters of the sun stood among them,

radiant, rooted in grief, their wind-sprung leaves
drifting toward a river no one would remember
were it not for the light trembling in the trees.

Playing Catch With the Dogwood

All summer the dry branches
crack and fall, scatter
on the lawn. I pile them
at garden's edge

and every day there are more. As long
as the wind has breath there are
more. The dog wants to play.
He is blue, and a rascal for afternoons.

Red and Its Biographer

—after Billy Collins

I picture red's biographer at his desk,
hunched over, writing incendiary prose
by candlelight. The manuscript begins

with red's humble entrance
into the visible spectrum, a low wave,
and covers its rise to a primary color.

Red, of course, is amused
by the attention, but remains aloof.
The biographer, who's amassed tomes

on dancing shoes, dresses, the nature of desire,
is a shy man who keeps to himself,
a shut-in in his little cabin. He seldom

angers, and would remain sexually
inert were it not for lingerie
catalogs. If red had its say,

it would have preferred a Plutarch,
Boswell, or even Jack Miles
to this wisp of a man. Ah, but winter

promises to be long and cold
and there is a warm fire here.
Red might stay for a while,

nudging now and again
when the text becomes too dull
and colorless.

Why There is Always a Ball in Their Water Dish

It's *Monday Night Football,*
cat-style. One jumps on the newel post,
a green or purple fuzz-ball dangling
from his clamped mouth
small mouse, cheap
toy stolen from my daughter's craft kit.
The other waits
for the leap, the chase
down the stairs, the lift
from the rug
on the mezzanine—*all air, baby!*—
the chase and eventual takedown
downstairs. There are a few
punches thrown, a few words exchanged.
One of them snatches up the ball
and takes off again.
It's all about time
of possession, technique,
knowing when to turn back, rising
like a bear behind a blind corner.
They are lucky to be alive,
these brothers, found
orphaned in a field, only
three days old and still
blind and deaf and mewling
for mother, who'd been struck
by a car. But they are
of Midwestern stock, hardy
boys with a lineage
of barns in their blood, a history
of sidling, and stalking mice.
It's there in the muscle memory,
the twitch of haunch
and tail, pursuit and pursued,
in the slotted aperture
that opens in celebration
of Now, the bood-
race, iambic pulse of
the game *the* game *the* game.

Rummage Sale

The Evel Knievel doll is not happy.
His box is cramped, and the RV is in a horrible state
          of disrepair.

He was never all that sure about the plastic-toothed
          thing that made his motorcycle rev, and the ramp
          was entirely at a wrong angle to leap the RV,
but he'd learned to live with these things. It was all part of the package.

          True, he was a little jealous of GI Joe's boat,
that gorilla, the flippers and scuba gear, all those cool guns and gadgets,
but he was Evel Knievel, after all, a daredevil by trade, the Elvis of the air.

Now, his shirt is stained,
and there is a piece of masking tape on his chest—
a few numbers, far less than a dollar.

It could be worse, he supposes.
In the next box, a Barbie lies prostrate
on a pile of books, pinpricks covering
the sexless region between her legs.

What he wouldn't give to be able to leap through the air again,
for the aching in his bones to stop for good,
and for just a few moments to hold Barbie in his arms
and tell her they could do worse than leave
where they are not wanted.

The Day the Funk Arrived

Just bring the funk
—Ben Harper

It came rolling over the horizon,
tumbling over itself in its
big-ass need
to bring the kingdom.
Cripples threw down their crutches,
hips seized with the push-pull swing
of planets and their satellites.
Boardrooms were boarded up,
meetings put on ice,
and the lords of the twenty-seventh floor
came down to the people,
strutting like street cats
with their balls to the wind.
The heavies came out swinging
their big backyards, carving
whole alphabets in the air.
The broken down and eaten up
got up and danced
like lambs among the lions.
It was a real resurrection party,
the whole city thumping
to the fat rhythm of bass and horns.
The funk was passing through.
That's right, the funk, motherfucker.
In a great big ship of glittering
stars. The funk. And a dashboard
of yellow fur.

The Pasta Bar

Friday nights, the jazz man, bass man
anchors the band, while the old black
piano man makes the whites and blacks
dance on an old upright. He lays down
those swinging keys, whole neighborhoods
of color for the saxes' dusty wails; *oh, yeah,*
and they're smoking, man, throwing hell
to the breeze, even the laid-back guitarist
rifling his meandog riffs; and all of them,
all of them, like a train rattling on the tracks,
all of them just a *clackety-yack* background
for fettuccini, bacon and peas.

The Anarchists in the Coffee Shop

—after G.E. Patterson

the anarchists
sprawled out
cigarettes glowing
in the near-dark
are never late for appointments
and believe life
is war

in the coffee shop
in the near-dark
angry
are anarchists
they have dangerous aesthetics
can't be deferred
and they believe in something

these good students
Martens propped up on chairs
cups filled with coffee
yes, are anarchists who
despite good parents
believe life should be
explosive

The People Up There

How could they have smuggled in,
past the desk clerks,
all those crates of circus elephants?
There's a godawful thump
and some dragging
and it must be them moving in
the trapeze and the strong man's cannon,
the crate for the rare white
anaconda. I hear the snap
of the tuba player's case,
the sloppy *ratchet-ratchet-ratchet*
of the drummer tightening his snare.
Soon-after: silence.
Then come the clowns, honking
their horns and tripping
over big floppy feet. Children
laugh while old men walk
the aisles, hawking
sno-cones and popcorn,
cotton candy and toys. I know—
am quite sure, in fact—this
will go on for much of the night,
so when my name is called,
I don my slip-ons
and climb up the taut cable
up and up, into
a darkness so complete
my way would be obscured
were it not for a thin cone
of light. Soon I am so high
I can almost step out of myself
and into thin air: arms
outstretched, Christ-like, jaw
chiseled in shadow.

When I reach the end, applause
come rolling over me
like a soughing of wind in the pines.
I am gracious, and bow deeply:
because it is expected,
and because I do not want
to climb back down
to the middle-aged man
grinding his teeth, far below,
in sleep.

Drought

This year fall arrived with a brutal cry,
withered stalks browning in untended fields,
brittle weeds all but hollowed, dust kicked up
by devils—still the cyclopean eye interrogates,
unafraid as it is, to burn.

But in the cool shadow of the highway bridge,
the ripple-platter of cars sounds like rain overhead.
All along the banks of the Mississippi,
insects buzz and chirrup, the weeks nearing
when they'll either die or burrow into the cold ground.
When snow crusts the hills, the bees
who now kiss the wildflowers with such abandon
will be hunkered in the hive, living
off the land's last gold.

The Dream of the Burning City

Great sheets of fire danced down the streets,
a parade of heat
seeking the inner chambers, where we could be found

hiding. We did all we could to escape,
but there would be no more running
from the veil of undoing. Tokens,

to be sure, we freed the small birds
of affection kept in cool basements,
carefully tended by loss.

III

The Ghost Town at Tinton

Black angus low to the dark hills
where men once slogged home from the mine
grimed with dirt and gold, loaded
with stories from twelve hours
in the hole. It is cooler now,
the sun a burnished orange over the berm.
Their bellows shiver down spearfish canyon.
Dark as shadows they wend
dirt paths between arthritic homes
kneeling in the grass, past
the old Ford rusting on a rise
flecked with mica, past
the post office and dance hall ruins
at main street's end, straddling
two states. Though the gold is gone,
the ground gives up tantalite ore
for missiles and consumer electronics,
metal that resists corrosion. Nights
like this, when all is still, sounds carry
for miles. Voices from a radio left on
on the top of a ridge can travel
through trees, too indistinct for love
or loss, and sift like ghostly fingers
through rotting walls where newspapers
fifty years old were once stuffed
to keep out the chill.

Nocturne

Down from the moist air
a brood on far limb folds
leathery wings, theirs

a sympathetic world built
from the echoes of the given.
There is talk of sleep

but sleep is elsewhere.
The rugs in God's outer chamber
are full of luminous beggars

speaking with tongues
of pale light. Silver foxes
wait in the ink-blue

afterimage of moon,
hungry for moles, willing to learn
and relearn where the doors

in the labyrinth are.
Crook-necked owls hoot
about the lesser concerns

of meadows and barns.
The eyes of tubers
grope through damp loam

like the gnarled fingers
of a root witch, reading
the rich Braille of earth.

For All I Know

poetry slips out of the lizard brain at night
unfettered from its cage of words
hungry and slippery with fire
gliding along the ground like a shadow
voiceless and soundless
full of the soundtrack of semen and blood
rising to its full height, it becomes shadowy and watchful
and wherever it sees there becomes a city
and there in the city are people
and all of the people are dreaming
and all of their dreams are about wakeful things
and these wakeful things make the cities
move and undulate like heat waves on asphalt
when it returns again and becomes
leashed in its dark cave
there it grows, unbearably
into a cool, white
flower

Fog, Bus

—after Charles Olson

On foggy mornings, the world
    unveils itself   from the center

        out,
as though to feign a sense of newness
    of just-appearing
of having slogged through that little slice of death
        we call sleep. This

gauzy curtain   floats   over the city,
    like the prestidigitator's sheet over
        half-glimpsed buildings
moored in ether.

Sounds, too, are disguised,
    object- and soulless, as if from another world
under   or   outside of
        ours.

The bus terminal,
        where you are,
    is the new center
        (as a locus, a focal point is)

strange in its newness: a permeable membrane whose borders
    are clouds built from last night's rain
and warm wind, the air
        saturated and heavy,
        a container.

There is the road, bricked and familiar, curving,
    but eaten edgeless.

                When the bus

        finally   appears

you experience a sense of déjà vu.

Could it be that you have died?

This particular bus (light's emissary)
is like all those you have ridden,
formerly,

but what proof have you that this transport
has not been conjured by mere desire?

If you knew that you were to be guided
across the gray erasure,

would you board?

Would you be ready for the light,
knowing its deep hunger,
its singular ability to swallow you whole?

Fire Tower

You could see four states
from the top; at least
that's what the ranger said.
My dad and I climbed
wide metal stairs that screwed
into the sky, each landing
fitted with a rusty rail.
We talked about nothing,
as always, but the world
I'd inherit, smoke
and steel, middle-aged men
working the graveyard
shift on the assembly line.
Past the trees, the world below
seemed daubed in paint,
less real somehow, unsteady
in the sway. Halfway up,
he raised a hand and would go
no further, overcome
with vertigo. Thirty years
later, I'm waiting for the bus
at the university, reading
of a girl climbing lighthouse
stairs in the dark. She steps
on stone, I step on steel.
The world, or what's become
of it, groans, a system
of bolts and braces, load
bearing beams, distance.
The look on my father's face:
not fear, exactly, but what,
disappointment? Why can't
I summon the memory of
the earth's ponderous curve,
the pale blue lightening over
a wide expanse of fields
and mountains, rivers
like fingers grayed by height?
Surely you would remember

a tableau like that all your life;
imagine, the swaying tower,
breathless, steel thrumming
like a live thing through
your feet, your hair whipping
your face; at such a sight
one might even believe in
the unity of all things,
least of all father and son.
Soon the girl will enter
the room where light pierces
fog. I shift, searching
for more; there is nothing.
His eyes, so beautiful
and blue, have become sky,
and the bus, so long in coming,
has arrived.

"In every boy child there is an old man dying"

but he doesn't feel the inhabitation yet,
only a sense of light as possibility—
rooms like vessels that hold the familiar
vase of lilacs and dandelions picked
for mother, the plink of water striking water
in bowls stacked precariously in the sink.
Beyond the sloping lawn: the field
where all manner of beasts lie
concealed in milkweed, bull thistles
and bunch grass, paths of dirt
like a trace of old veins between.
And parked in the dead end, a man
idly watches, unfiltered cigarette taking
the slow trip from car window to lip.

In certain circumstances, it might be months
before they find the boy's body,
snow packing then melting in the ravine.
With light low over the sodden grass,
volunteers might remark on the shoe,
how close it was. But the boy is tugged
by doubt. He stops mid-field and
gathers stones to take home and paint.
Someday he'll forget everything but the cast
of his body, how he stood, hand curled
around stone. The stone? A faded blue
now, like a small face staring up
from the bottom of a long lost box.

Still Life, With Mother

She washes dishes by hand now
so she can stand
in the light at half-dark
and look out on the yard. Her hands
                    go down into the water,
                    float like pale flounder
                    in the murk. She brings up
                    a plate, washes round the rim as
a crow wings down
from its circuit, nightly habit
of checking in. Its eyes are black
points, bereft of emotion, a pointillist's
                    suggestion of sight. What is left
                    now but the exercise
                    of the common, motions known
                    by rote, the familiar
claim on life. There beside
the cutting board is the knife.
Every day she tells herself
that one more day is enough.

This Man

There is no food before him.
No drink, napkin or straws.
Just a man off the street,
with nothing else to do.

"No," he says, "that's a shame,"
and shakes the daily paper.

He might be an angel,
one of Rilke's, perhaps,
though less terrifying
in runnels of long dirty hair
and tattered, stained coat.

In a mote of light,
he's scans the obituary,
looking for names he knows.
Could it be he's sent
to preside over a tragedy?

When he looks up,
he seems to mark you with eyes
scarred and luminous from war;

looking closer, you see
they are fixed somewhere
over your head.

Second-Shift Fathers

By these signs you will know them, those
who come and go like ghosts,
who sleep through the morning, snoring like bears

in rooms of dead air and shade.
You will know them
by their hard black lunch pails unsnapped

on the counter. The lunchmeats in the fridge, wrapped
in butcher paper: off-limits.
Their work shirts are ripped or hacked

at the sleeves, burned
with bullet holes from the sparks of contact
welders. No nonsense shoes stand

on a rug by the back door, wormy laces
drooped with fatigue. You may find them
sleeping on hallway floors

on Sunday afternoons, when an air
of after-church lassitude drifts like a spirit
through the house. If you do

find them in these attitudes, they will have
their arms draped over their eyes, chests
rising and falling like oxygen pumps.

Though nocturnal by nature, you might
glimpse one or two furtively dashing
to the hardware store for nine-penny nails, or

the auto store for a fuel pump
to be installed on Saturday (when they will lie
on a dolly in the drive, transistor radio parked

on the porch). Listen to me:
some of the fathers believe
in the power of dreams, their ability

to predict the future. Some,
like small boys, still see blue angels burning
streaks in the sky. Most hold space

in their mind for an island on the other side
of the planet, a balls-out one-ton truck,
or high-definition TV. They return to their homes

after thirty years in the plant only to find
their children grown and the floor sagging
under the weight of the walls. If their roofs leak

they climb ladders and sit for a smoke, watching
the families up the street. They touch themselves
in the mirror, if only

to feel the thin skin, how it covers the bones
like tissue. They walk about the house in the dark,
before the sun comes up, when there is

nothing but a westbound train lowing
from a faraway field. They wait for the telltale signs
the world is waking up, for the birds to roll over

in their nests and greet the day the only way
they know how. Then the second-shift fathers
do what they have always done. They climb back in bed,

lock down the coffin lid, and wait for that old enemy,
the day, to arrive, tripping over itself with gladness,
and holding a bouquet of yellow roses.

Reunion

You don't see them for so long
and then you do. It's like visiting your old town
and though everything looks the same it's aged,
different enough to seem strange.
Everyone is talking about this or that
person—some you know, most you don't—
and how many years they've been in the grave.
The farmers talk about *the old place,*
the farm *back in the day,* when the orchards
were still damp and the barns
were filled with the smells of sweet hay
and cow manure, spilled milk in the milkhouse
and silage. Your cousin, whom you've not seen
in twenty years, is talking about spearfishing
at a low point in the river, hunting
for mushrooms in the woods where he found
a score on the backside of an ash,
and rebuilding a good engine.
His life seems so far removed from yours
you wonder what it would be like
to grow up in his skin, to live
close to the earth, your roots.
Where you are its been raining for days.
The soil is muddy and loose.
When the straight-line winds come, the trees
are torn out of the earth and laid in the streets,
one after the other, like straw.

Night Call

—for Chip Nelson

Mother said she was sorry, but was calling because there'd been an accident. She wanted me to hear of my friend's death from a familiar voice. "A drunk driver," she said. "A doctor." I dressed as if in a slow dream and went down to wander the dark streets. Sometime later—it might have been minutes, it might have been hours—I heard reggae, and followed the sound back to an open window. I sat on the curb to listen. The night was warm and there was a slight breeze, a hint of morning in the sky. It seemed as though something wonderful had come and gone, a carnival perhaps. I'd arrived late, but at least there was still music.

Another Kind of Resurrection

I remember how your long white hair
flowed like water

down to your waist, rivulets
over the bed of a beaten leather jacket.

I thought you must be some kind of river god,
not a guitar player

or a hard drinking Norwegian
who loved Jesus and a good fight.

It didn't help much that I was only seventeen,
face blistered with pimples.

My arms and legs were like nervy ganglions
I could barely control.

I saw how easily girls came to you,
how you would cast them off with a boyish shrug.

I wondered why they forgave you
and kept coming back.

So I learned to play. Really play.
Cloistered in my room with books

splayed out on the bed,
I learned the caged system, and the Segovian,

the augmented and diminished scales,
pentatonic and blues. I drew

time-lapse pictures of my hair growing—
three-months, six months, two years—

while time folded itself
into the sound of a crowd,

that murmuring gathering of water you can hear
from backstage.

I say this now because you've been gone
for fifteen years, and I've been thinking about the angel

holding the scepter of fire over your head,
the angel you talked about that night

at the Blackbridge Bar as we knocked back
burning shots of Yukon Jack and Rumpelminze

in a contest to see who would last the longest.
Sometime after midnight, you pulled me close and told me

you were called by God
to raise a band with spiritual powers.

You wanted to heal the sick,
have the power to raise the dead.

But you were a man, and even then
you were already dying.

When you pulled out from the stop sign that May,
did you sense the nearness of death

behind the wheel of the drunken dermatologist's Ford?
Did you look out the car window

and think, *Shit I'm going to die*
just like my old man. I'd like to believe you laughed

at the irony of it, the flick
of a second before impact.

While this is not exactly a scepter of fire,
know that this small wraith of flame

is raised in your honor, blue
at the core, like water.

Fever

The shivering comes
                    from the center of your soul,
rocks the frame, rattles the windows
                    and the bones.

There is nothing
                    like this paint-blistering flame
to make the house
                    so with desire and loss ache,

as smoke moves
                    from room to room seething
like a winnowed ghost
                    in a dream of former being.

When the visions come,
                              those blurred and lurid,
three-eyed and serpent tailed things
                              wrenched

from some private darkness,
                              remember the roar
and crackle of the fire.
                              Your body is not your

own, but some badly rendered,
                              nervy, sack of blood,
achy muscle and bone
                              hovering in a heat-haze 101.

When your fever breaks
                              and you are told it is time
to go, smile, and don't take your eyes
                              off the lion.

For Sale by Owner

White rattle-trap coughing black smoke
like clouds of creosote out the back,
quarter panels riddled with rust,
frame strip-mined of metal,
the whole jalopy widdle-waddling
down the highway on balding tires.
Slunk low behind the wheel,
twisted like the frame from an old accident:
the frowsy-haired driver.
He nods. *Carrying on, brother.*
At the mill, a windowless sweltering box
smelling of sweat, wool, and diesel fumes,
he threads bags of fiber
spit out from carding machines.
The foreman is a cranky son-of-a-bitch
out from jail on a work furlough;
like a rodent, he emerges from his corner office
once an hour to survey the floor
and turn up the speed on a few machines.
If you are unlucky enough to work
the floor, you can seem him grinning from his hole,
gray hair dancing from a desktop fan.
Having punched out for the day,
the man is heading home to a pepperoni pizza
and a six-pack of Old Milwaukee.
As the evening slowly settles,
he'll leave the lights off in his apartment
and sit before the window fretting
chords on a Les Paul goldtop.
He'll think of Cincinnati,
Minneapolis, Madison—all those
Midwestern towns, the years he believed
in chance. His reflection, in the deepening dusk,
grows darkly luminous, like an X-ray
of lungs. *Has new battery. Runs.*

Nuclear Medicine

The angel has grown weary.
No one has made a run for eternity
since the days when the garden was young,
and the effort to stand ready
has made him mortal.

Bodies on white-sheeted gurneys
are lined up in the house of fear:
an old man, placid, nearly transparent;
a baby in a plastic tub, eyes taped shut,
tubes running along both arms;
others, spilling into the hallway
like oil at the scene of an accident.

In the lounge four hours later,
a boy watches TV, shivering
beneath a blanket. A nurse pops in
to ask how he is doing. He ignores her.

A man who's pissed a toilet bowl full of blood
watches from the corner, wondering
whether the boy has just had a dose
or is merely cold from the air circulators
and the press of long hours.
He will come back soon,
and has already begun to practice
naming shadows.

Another Poem About the Dead

The dead are tired of translations.
They carry their lives in typesetter's drawers,
honeycombed rooms packed with miniatures of the moon.
Postcards of a cat staring after the tide, long braid of water
necklacing sand. A porcelain matador, hands wiped clean
of bull blood, smiles for a crowd. In another summer,
it was Paris and the Tour Montparnasse; now a bullet-sized
Eiffel Tower stands in the tray for capital M's.
There are no Polaroids of midnight trips to the toilet,
no vomit on the rug or pills in a cup marked *Monday*.
Sneaking through these chambers, the dead bear their stories
to draughty back rooms, where for a scotch and a smoke
they'll unpack rumors of their lives.

Easter Remembrances

—from Josef Sudek's photograph of the same name

A smooth egg in a smooth bowl
on a weather-beaten, cracked and chafed sill:

These white curves—
    so much the engine of the unmoved mover—

resting now   reflective
as though there were something to be said
about seeing oneself be still
and at odds with decay.

Diastole

i.)

The old jazz drummer's hands pop and jerk
on the pew—

...pa, badda, be bop,
bah dah, badda, be bop...

His head lolls, canted as an egret preening
in the dark
orange minute before sunrise.

Hallelujah!

A girl steps through the door
of Wal-mart
and twirls, her shirt sparking with light.

Her younger sister, betrayed by beauty,
covers her mouth,
and the long war between them stalls.

Amen!

A wolf spider rappels from the railing
of a paddleboat steamer on a hot afternoon.

Soon it will begin the task of assembling a sail.

ii.)

The sky is angry and yellow.

The transistor radio crackles, jazz
flits in and out.
"Stay tuned," a thin voice says,
and the lights flicker

and die. Outside, the wind raises its hackles.
    Sirens wail.
Hail tattoos the window.

The little girl, huddling with hands over ears,
    hears her blood *whoosh*
like the rinse-cycle of a washing machine.

Twenty years later she will remember this night,
laundering clothes in graduate school.

iii.)

There is a rhythm in our days.

This is what we learn after we have been cut
    and cut again.

When you have reached the edge of your endurance,
    stop the car. Listen
to the hot engine tick, the blood rush of cars on the road.

Lift your face as you did when you were young
and running was everything.

IV

Game Day

The blue doors open.
The room fills with contrails.

Leaping, fish
forget their names, at the apex believe
in the arc of flight. Mountains
slowly pace along the sidelines, their beautiful jaws clenched
in anticipation.

The engines are at home this time.
Everyone is buzzing. The woods wag their fingers
of praise, speak
in the tongues of wind and seeds.

It is another day of light
carting its little wagon of tears over crushed glass.

Another day of flowers
staring at their jagged reflections.

At dusk
the girl made of wood
becomes light and smoke, heat
uncoiling
with whispers and whorls
in the deep cul-de-sacs, in the heartwood,
where the god of ash whistles.

The black doors close.

A fox watches from wood's-edge, eyes flashing
with caution.

Clouds unfold their dark hands,
present an audience of lights.

Tomorrow,
the engines travel, so tonight
they are thrumming
under the hoods of sleep.

The Swimmer

Air pools with the sound of water.

Under undulating light a figure
sluices arm over head, hand

cupped, pulling
for tighter form, a few seconds shaved.

It is the rhythm
of breath and swing, body

arrowing edge to edge, against time.
Against weight. Not the self

dreaming, not
the somnambulist's feel for wall, or

the day returning, eyeless, lidless
as ghost fish in the greater deep.

It is the act of becoming
myth. The drawn breath, face pressed

to water. The arm lifting,
water arcing in release. Now, the ease

of slipping into the turn, the push
and kick toward surface

where light waits. Toward hands held
open, the burst of welcome.

Two Births

Came into the world
blue, reedy voice railing
                    at light, having burst
my husk of blood,
a seed pressed through bone.

The first piece
is always the hardest to find
among the turned trees and bricks
            mortared
    in sun. An edge and a corner,
the home appears. Further,
    a context
    of spires. And then the shift:

waves, a fishing boat chased
by a cloud of screaming gulls,
    jib and sail (the whole sky, really)
    mostly unmade among

those questions still on the table.

    Ringing. A partial,
flash and afterimage—

that push,
that curve toward the surprising
    violence of light. And me: holding
        my single silver coin, still

covered in the fluids of travel, my eyes
glittering
    like winter in a kingdom of rust.

Something Like Quiet

There is a small house behind my left eye.
The man who lives there enjoys keeping bees.
He and his wolfhound sometimes stand on the bluff
overlooking the sea. The sea sounds very far away.
His name is Michael or Matthew—
something that starts with "M" anyway.
He likes to look at the clouds far off over the water.
Then he puts on his keeper's mask and walks among
the bees, humming. He likes that his humming
is drowned by the bees droning. The buzzing
is reassuring. He walks slowly among them,
as though in an oven, a shining man.
The dog does not go with him when he walks
in the cloud of bees. The cloud of bees
is a place he must go alone. When he returns
there is something like quiet between them.
In the evenings he returns to the bluff
with his dog. He thinks about an identical man
in an identical house on the other side of the sea.
If there is a pinprick of light far out over the water,
as there sometimes is, he believes the other man
is performing miracles. He wonders what there is
to see out there, with nothing but water and sky.

The Neon Fish

As if the whole thing could be understood at once
she paused and looked into her bag for her private things.
The world rotated into some new kind of perspective,
some new kind of light, and all the old things were forgotten.
Something came up from the bottom,
glittering like the deepest fish,
and found itself away from home in the lessened pressure.
The puzzle is never really complete, is it?
It's not like the picture will hold still.
Yes, there is the lipstick and the mirror.
Africa will remain affixed to the globe.
Snow will fall and tomorrow will come, indelibly.
She will open her eyes and the gentle gray light
will bring something new.
What does it all mean, moving through the day,
through the striped rhythm of shadows?

Hebridae

Velvet bug,

sphagnum bug,

mini-christ on water –

your swift-moving legs, the cogs
of my imagination. How rightly the eye

gathers there
on the blue lip, where the tension
of your legs divides the inner world
from the outer,

your act no less miraculous for its balance

than how the mind casts its eye
into that saucer of blue skin,
touches the living motor,
moves over

the inverse of clouds and into the air,

becomes a jet stitching the sky.

The Press of Small Hours

This evening, with its dim birth –
    a train lowing
in a star-plucked field, cold
having uncoiled, the dark ratcheted-in.

It is January, the very beast of winter,
    and I'm descending,
        gear for gear,
into the engine of silence.

    So it is,
I forage for a new suit of skin, a translation
    of myself that can survive
    anything.
I pace the house, full of the bee-buzz

and static of aloneness, the dark speaking
    in tongues. Before morning,
my limbs will have become light-strewn, fire-blown,

flowered with nebulous gasses:
rent into colors,
    the idea of light
before it explodes with meaning. But there is

the press of small hours before then
    and the night,
        with its doll face and old eyes,
is brittle and still as a held breath.

On Poetics

If, under the aegis of dead men,
you see obsolescence, celebrate
the gas's cold compression in the balloon. If

the experiment fails, you may have to start near
the middle,
in the nursery of opinions.

Don't talk about the sky, for it is older
than conversation. Likewise the heart, thrashing in the ship's futtocks.
These are commercials for the moon.

In time—

the stars, chattering in the standing room, will stop grieving
for their sheen;
snakes will abandon their sexual terrorism;
wine will return
to a constellation of grapes.

I'm waiting in the pub, watching the dust sing madly
in the weighted light,
a latecomer to the ballyhoo.

What is Over, What is Nearing

The shadows came and cut it out—
                    all of it, including the roots—
and carted it off on flatbed trucks.

That was yesterday, while you watched from the window.

But today, ah! You've your desires to worry over.
                    The tiny cathedral hiding in your bedside drawer.
The toilet's rusty bridle. The frost on the demon box, etc.

After all these years the bronzed lovers have greened.
Even Damocles,

whose sleep was filled with the fear of coins, woke
overjoyed by lack.

So now: vigilance. For the engine's senile tick,
      the eggs' fragile torus:

                  mice dreaming of the perfect anti-cat salvo;

                          debris in the equations for strange attractors.

There and gone, erased. Redrawn. Even now
an asteroid, slung through the far heavens—

that muscled arc of coming, swing home of coming

that hammer.

Today at the Bureau of Joy

Revolutionaries took the minister of happiness hostage.
Young men, mostly, who tend to speak in one-minute parables
about the truth behind the pyramids on Mars. The sexual dynamism

of flowers. The zygote's original split from monism.
Change is hard to appreciate. We've all been there
when filaments pop and the maestro cues a new firmament.

Nothing's ever the same when the replacements come. Plastic threads
strip too easily, corners don't fit, and there can be a problem
of scale in the manual (see Fig. 1). At least we can rest well

knowing that all the offensive words have been substituted
for others that mean nearly the same thing. Ketchup, for instance,
has stopped being red, is a tomato-based paste again.

With a membership card, you can save if you buy in bulk.
The application is quick and painless, and requires
very little original thinking. You'll be glad you joined. Really.

Of course, the change seminars are mandatory; there'll be
the usual chances for small group interaction, and you'll need
to put away those photos of wingless fruit flies, but at least

you'll get a nice jar of lightning for your desk. Believe me, I know.
When breathing gets difficult, I walk to the river for inspiration.
The tortured water below the dam confesses nothing, reveals

no secrets. It swirls, faintly brown and yeasty, but is J2EE compliant.
That's something, isn't it? To build on, I mean. Not quite a story
for the papers, but then again, the simple pleasures rarely are.

Tuesday in the Wolf Factory

And all the wolves in the wolf factory, paused
for a moment of silence, at noon.
—John Ashbery

You've looked in your bag of windows and found the sun
glinting off the doors in the west wing. It's not quite so strange, you know,
that the grenades have become rubies. It's a one-time performance,
a sold out show. A prestidigitator's trick, perhaps, but slick as Cool Whip.
Observe: most of the crooked smiles have been straightened,
yet the straight smiles bend at right angles.

Starfish have been called in to arbitrate—a last minute affair, really—
flown in from the sea on chartered planes. There'll be no throwing them back
this time. It's all come down to a few words, and everyone is waiting
to see what will happen.

If you arch your back to look at the sky, you'll be surprised
by the power of flashlights. Pudding does that sometimes. Don't worry,
I've learned how to not-look, or rather, to pretend to not-see. Either way, it's easier
to stop splitting an infinitive than a few hairs. The stories are a little edgier
further East, but not so far East that it becomes West again.
Red Riding Hood, for instance, can mean any number of things.

So you want proof. Consider this: in this time of miracles
hair loss is not permanent. Teams of trained rats can save lives.
Yes, I know, you can read as well as anyone—the question is, which losses
are important? If the nouns are not in agreement with the verbs
then I wash my hands of everything. We'll leave it all to the talking cabbages
for analysis. The less we know about the making of Swiss cheese, for example,
the easier it will be to sleep at night.

The Anatomy of Echolocation

The rapscallions have painted their doors red.
It was decided in private, unanimously, by a group show of hands
in what was, perhaps, the single largest unrecorded demonstration
of non-conformity ever. It's so hard to get it all together, sometimes—
Lord knows, the balloons don't always cooperate. There are corporations
to consider, crepuscular corpuscles of cinnamon and spice,
towers of avarice and sand. It's not always the same thing
on a different day, sometimes it's a different thing on the same day.
A different story with the same plot. Clearly, things have got to change.
The right hand doesn't talk to the left, and nobody proofreads
the stars anymore. It's no one's fault, exactly.
We just aren't sure if anyone is there, that's all.

Our findings were surprising, though. Right now, for example,
outside 4 out of 5 households, bats are beaming their own brand of rock-n-roll,
but they're pirated programs broadcast with a weak signal.
If you think about it, the night is more than a game of cloak and dagger,
spilled bottles of ink, blueberries and the absence of light. Grains of sand
worry in their muscular beds. Lace yellows. Flowers yelp for attention
in sandy swales. Yes, the formula is there for the right ear.
All it takes is the right moment and the ability to listen deeply,
the way you do when looking at a hologram. But not really.

Look, it was just here. If we keep looking for it, we're bound to find it.
No matter what the wave experts say, sine matters. It's a fact of life.
The trick is to hang up before the telemarketers call back.
It will give the maids something to talk about. They're the ones, after all,
who tuck in our empty sheets and leave mints on our pillows.
If they don't believe in our secret lives, who will?

The Shrike in the Garden of Machinery

i.)

A lesser god in the kingdom of thorns,
I carried Eve out of storage
one sleepless night, plucked her eyes
from their case, oiled her rusty joints.
By lamplight, I planned to remake her
from memory, a goddess before good and evil,
the original Conversation. All that.

I blew the dust from her hair,
set the torsion of her fingers,
wound the key in her back. Why?
To watch her mouth bloom. So I could,
as a drunken bee, buzz at her lips.
I wanted her to speak to me, undress
with conviction. But she was dead. Folded
into the book of days like a flier for happiness.

ii.)

Isn't this is the way of things? Clematis flowers
sprouting and rotting on the same angry vine. The one thing
you can't have centered in your mind, a splinter.

The clot of traffic, those in the city drowning
on sidewalks. The improvisation of ventricles,
dilated pupils. Hours dreaming the perfect *Thing*.

Portrait of man leaning toward window.
Man waiting for bus. Man wedged in slices of bread.
A refrain: *one day the next day the day before...*

It won't be long before the hatchling pecks
through the skin of that building, and that, emerging
wet and weak-necked, sport for a new breed of man.

And still there is the hunt for the Fruit.
The blood of erasure. The Serpent's belly rasping
on steamy roadside grates. *Do you know, yet,*

the price of knowledge? There in the center of it all,
the spike, the compass lined with bodies.

iii.)

Listen. There are three ways to speak.
One involves hiding in the weeds, covered

with stories. Though you may be tempted to,
don't call me Adam. I've never been here before.

I come out of the redness of earth.
My eyes are on fire.

The solid weight of the Pomegranate is a real thing.
Everything else is a mnemonic for desire.

Many Names for the Monkey

Tota. In certain lights, is green.
Like the lava lamp that sat atop his grandma's TV,
toxic clouds *rising sinking rising* like some alien
time piece. For hours he would watch
the blobs metamorphose in that eidolic glow,
encapsulated in slow-moving silence.
It seemed like a kind of time behind
time, a waiting in aloneness, as he'd sense again
with a forkful of food hovering before his mouth;
he'd forget how it got there and how to make
his arm move. There was nothing to do,
it seemed, but wait for time to catch up to itself.
In that time of absolute stillness he discovered
that the light knew his name. He and it
were alive, and part of the same source.

Grivet. Black residue is packed in tinfoil balls
wadded around the trailer. The days have become
a rhythm of *filling emptying filling,* light
appearing and disappearing in the window
like the stills of a zoetrope. He thinks about
container and *thing-contained,* a complement
of purpose. The nature of waiting. The manifold
of space and time a strong will could annul.
His clothes droop on hangers in the closet,
soldiers too fatigued to enter the day.
He leaves only for food, is astonished
by the brilliance of daylight, how tiring is
the swing and plod of his legs. The point
is the trip, a reconnaissance. Wiseman entering
the clearing, where the future still burns.
Apocalyptic village. Wiseman waiting
for instructions. For revelation.

Vervet. Masquers along the avenue
wine-drenched in their bacchanal, midnight lit
with revel. The monkey's face is unreadable
now, disguised by night. You can't see
the hands over his eyes, for they are black.
Likewise his ears and mouth. Death is
24-hours from any place on earth. *Marburg, ebola.*
That woman, that man, dressed as a pig,
eyes wild with fear. Blood pouring
from every pore. *The life is in the blood.*
Elsewhere, eremites come out of clay-packed caves
wearing only diadems of weeds and ash,
uttering the monkey's ancient name.
He huddles in the trees, moveless as a gargoyle,
green backpack slung into the branches
full of all that is holy.

Three Angels, a Door, and the Moon

In the beginning an angel
carried an anvil out of heaven

and set it in the burning meadow.
On one curved and indurate arm

he hammered anguish into ice and ice into sky,
pausing only to wipe blood from his eyes.

A second angel cracked the window
to jack-wedge the sun into place.

A third upended a bowl of clouds.
Out of a river of bones sprang

the jerboa and steppe wolves,
terns and tigers – all

the dusty beasts of justice,
as-yet-unmolested by mites, etc.

This was the end of the age of desire
and the beginning of representation.

Now an old wooden door has rotted for centuries
in the musty basement of the rainbow.

Beyond it lies the pitted face of the moon,
a globe of ash and minor light. It weeps

every twenty-eight days, when its dish
of candy for the sea is empty.

V

Where Nothing Grows

[1]

The parking lot is strewn
with the wreckage
of pumpkins, burned wood

and glass, the air
a mizzling white a-blur
with the wings of doves

fighting for pulp and mash.
If I believed in signs, I'd say
this promises to be a day of need.

I move through the hours
with an eye to the glass, watching
cars scuttle by on the freeway

lambent in headlights.
The office windows tick
with sleet. Heat kicks on

while my cursor blinks—
on*off* on*off*—as though stunned.
I watch workers wilt

on the bus home, their heads
sagging in the harsh light
like poisoned dandelions.

[2]

There wasn't always this evenness
of middling light, or cold air with its brace

of winter coming. Just yesterday
there were wraiths bluing the soft lips

of wild night gardens. Woods brimmed
with strange music and slow fires, ecstasy.

There was always time – so much time –
for birth and rebirth, for the bees

to hum in the orchards, drowsy
with sweet-rot and sun; always time

to hold the sky by its drawstring
while clouds drifted over green fields

swallowed in slow-moving shadows;
time to build and destroy

and rebuild again just for the sheer joy
of being the demiurge. No one

believed in the death of faith, or
an end, much less the long death beyond.

[3]

The body has been at war with itself
since the first separation:
from Mother, with a lusty

yowl in the bright-lit cold
of a new room; from Spirit,
gloved in a raiment of skin.

It calls to itself in strange tongues,
says *enemy*, says *other*
and walks in the rubble

carrying the war dead, the
children charred in their play clothes.
It reaches into the dust

for the jawbone of an ass, angered
at the right hand, the hipbone
and the eye. It has known

a beginning it cannot remember,
and will know an end
it cannot see, days filled

with calumny, enmity, hands
clutching rocks, eyes lifted
skyward for the first signs of rapture.

[4]

But where is heaven? In a hollowed
pomegranate, bubbling

on a spoon? Secreted, perhaps,
in a lacquered box with gold filigree.

A kept mistress. A new loft
built in the scooped-out belly

of the old river mill. Even now,
in the year of cranes, the tower cranes

are lined up, jibs pointing past
mounded dirt piebald with snow.

And there is a fence, always a fence,
separating the new from the old.

And here, where the theater will be,
there is one also. On one side, lighted

signs and the concrete blocks that daily
rise like castle walls out of the ashes

of time. On the other, the lot
where the homeless drink, flushed

from the woods by cold
and a clear view of retreat.

Some mornings only refuse remains,
a garbage can dragged

from the park, blackened
by fire. Smashed glass, frost-covered

and yellowed by lamps, twinkling
like stars in the hard-packed snow.

It makes me wonder if time does not
exist, as a mystic once suggested.

Maybe there are only small and grand
dramas, with their seeds of conflict.

[5]

Winter, with its top-down lock
on dimension, its
insistence on black-and-white,
is a time of consideration, of cold
felt as a slowing of blood, the blood
pulling back into the fact
of itself, circular
as the earth's currents
in the slip of rotation, powered
by the same engine
that makes two four, forms
the heart and lungs, and stars
out of gaseous clouds.

In the beginning was the Word,
and the word was a name
and the name held the *thing,*
as *saucer* does its infinite home
for *cup.* But what are *things,* exactly,
when all is translated, inverted,
traveling as signals into
the brain, some Mind, not
as things-in-themselves
but things-as-they-are-perceived?
What would it mean to doubt,
except, on the level of sign?

[6]

A blood-red cardinal descends,
wings outspread before a brilliant scrim

of snow. In the next moment
he will land and take what he needs, driven

by hunger and a gift of seeds.
For now I am content to leave him

in the air, a-blur:
a suggestion of coming–

The Line

—Sanibel Island's Gulf Coast

There where the blue meets blue
and water become vapor, there is a line.
It keeps the one from the other,
the lighter from the deeper blue.
Early, when the clouds are sleepwalking
and our eyes are coated with sleep, there is only one color:
a fabulous, light-rolling-dream-mist that obscures
all concerns with time and gravity.
As the day opens, the sun emerges in all its possessive glory,
draws the secret myths back into itself.
The water below breaks into song.
The water above rises and sails.
All that is blue returns to itself, knowing itself.
The line is clearly visible now, cloaked
in the strange assumption of difference.
To ask where it is, exactly, this line between heaven and earth,
is to invite the soul on a journey to find
what does not exist.

"Nothing, having arrived, will stay"

This delicate globe of pollen,
having fallen far from the flowering maple,
seems to hover on a warm shelf
of air. It rotates in sun, fibrous arc
a small horizon between buildings.

Doors open and close.
Under whirls and eddies of air
men and women, dressed in the language
of business, weave a thread in the whole-cloth
that is Monday. Above them,
around them, between them, the design
of all things made visible: limned
in light eight minutes out of
the engine of life.

All that is green turns, aching—
from window boxes, from mud-
washed and garbage-strewn alleys,
from fields and meadows—
for the reds, deep indigoes and violets.
In every cell a miniscule motor thrums
with an infinitive. And trailing not far behind,
the engine of decay, of forgetting,
of never was.

"more furious selves"

more fire than water or
when water rising

into atmosphere, into shape-
shifting fields of gray

a bomb
with a questionable detonator

sensitive to light, to
vibration, to

the slightest change
in pressure   the sound

of photosynthetic processes, the
multifarious prayers

of leaves unfolding, binary
states of bioluminescence—

night's ignition—
attraction, all the matters

of scale (as of)
the stem's fibrous ladder,

electrons' higher-order
escape from idea

and all these   and all these
repetitions, the ocean's mere

groping for shore, a pattern
of dissembling

the moon beyond this
mountain, this volcano, this

search for what is
fuel for the second stage,

the itch of ignition,
fire pushing

the pistons   the whole
machine lurching

out of stasis, the
latticework of capillaries

filling the wide
iris

So Much of X is Y

and I'm careless of the wind blowing
through the holes in my body, low whistle

of subterranean congress, fore-lit train
rising into a day buttered with promise. Careless

of infatuations with neon, wolf-hour
visions of the fifth angel polishing its trumpet

on the eve of destruction; the whip-tag tryst
of nerve and brain. Those things.

I am on fire, writing letters to the dead,
swallowing swords—anything to appease

the inventor of sorrow. Tomorrow
is a game of euchre with the ghost of midnight,

and I'm an odds-on favorite for resurrection.
Who knew it would feel this good

to run nude through butterflies?
The wind is filled with music,

a verse and chorus of birds, a trumpeting
of orange-flowered vine climbing lattice.

I'm watching the sky while ants march for shelter,
this itch the nose-burn of ozone,

curl of dog-lip and black tulips, careless
of skirling sirens. I've been here in dreams,

at the intersection of store-back and alley,
plastic and alloy, sweet tincture of key and chord.

This is where the song forms, rising out of nothing,
with little more than a few ideas about itself.

Notes

The following titles have been taken from lines of these poems:

"a small blue god" from "Here I am Walking," by Gerald Stern;

"Nothing, having arrived, will stay" from "The Slip,"
by Wendell Berry, later by Raymond Carver in "The Lightning Speed of the Past" ;

"In every boy child an old man is dying" from the section "Him" in "The Snowmass Cycle" by Stephen Dunn;

"more furious selves" from "Evening Without Angels" by Wallace Stevens

Printed in the United States
44518LVS00004B/58-78

9 780977 127290